YOU CAN NEVER BREAK ME

Overcoming Challenges, Building Resilience, and Thriving Against All Odds"

ROBIN J MARTIN

You can never break me

Overcoming Challenges, Building Resilience, and Thriving Against All Odds"

ROBIN J MARTIN

1

Chapter 1

Table of contents

2

Chapter 2

Introduction to the book

We all experience trials in life that put our strength, drive, and character to the test. Whether it's a personal loss, a professional setback, or a seemingly insurmountable hurdle, these experiences may either shatter us or expose our real resilience. "You Can Never Break Me" is a book about the human spirit's extraordinary ability to endure hardship and rise above life's most difficult difficulties.

You will go on a journey of self-discovery, empowerment, and change inside the pages of this book. We shall go into the depths of resilience, uncovering its core and investigating the numerous factors that contribute to its growth. Understanding and appreciating resilience can help you uncover the inner strength and steadfast fortitude you need to tackle any obstacle.

"You Can Never Break Me" strives to inspire and encourage you on your road to resilience via personal experiences, research- backed ideas, and practical techniques. Each chapter has been thoughtfully created to offer you useful skills and views that will enable you to not just survive but flourish in the face of adversity.

We'll start by setting the groundwork for resilience, delving into its meaning and value in our lives. We will investigate the power of mentality, learning how our ideas and beliefs impact our abilities to overcome obstacles. Then, we'll look at the skill of accepting adversity and seeing its possibilities for development and change.

As we go along, we'll uncover the main components that lead to inner strength, such as emotional resilience, stress management skills, and fostering self-compassion. We will also investigate the transforming power of perspective, learning how to adjust our perspectives and gain fresh insights in challenging circumstances.

We will highlight the value of personal resources throughout the book, such as recognizing and exploiting our abilities, developing a supporting network, and practicing self-care. We will also discuss the significance of resilience in relationships as we navigate effective communication, conflict resolution, and cultivating relationships that lift us through difficult times.

In addition, we will look at the importance of purpose in promoting resilience, and how connecting with our own goal may be a strong motivator. We will next go into the art of flourishing through change, learning how to adapt, accept ambiguity, and discover strength in transition.

Finally, "You Can Never Break Me" will end by delving into the extraordinary experiences of people who have conquered all obstacles and personified unbreakable spirits. Their stories will serve as a monument to the unlimited potential that exists inside each of us, inspiring readers to begin on their paths of resilience.

Remember, my reader, that no matter what challenges you face, you have an unbreakable spirit inside you. With each page flipped and lessons learned, you'll get closer to discovering your actual power. It's time to embrace your inner strength and understand that you can never break me.

3

Chapter 3

Resilience and Why It's Important for Success?

Have you ever wondered why some individuals can keep their cool in the face of hardship while others crumble? People who can successfully negotiate life's highs and lows have what psychologists call resilience, or the capacity to properly recover from adversity.

When confronted with a terrible circumstance, you have two options: allow your emotions to take over and become immobi- lized by dread, or raise yourself from the negativity and change pain into possibilities.

Even if you believe yourself to be a happy person, you will

certainly face difficulties along the way. These events may flex your muscles, but they do not have to break them.

Building resilience is essential for transforming obstacles into accomplishments.

We all can cultivate a resilient attitude; but, it must be conditioned and reinforced daily, much like a muscle. It is often necessary to reach your emotional barrier before you can access your resilience.

But what exactly is resilience? And why is it so critical to our success?

The concept of resilience originated in the 1970s in the realm of developmental psychopathology. Psychiatrists and psycholo- gists observed that a tiny proportion of youngsters with mental problems did not exhibit the usual maladaptive behaviors.

Instead, they exhibited social development characteristics that were within the usual range.

The study of children of schizophrenic parents, however, and the discovery that some children flourished despite their high-risk condition, led to the growth of resilience. These included a variety of negative circumstances, including socioeconomic deprivation, parental mental illness, mistreatment, disease, and catastrophic life events.

Resilience is proven to be a considerably more common phenomenon than previously imagined. The concept of resilience developed to assume substantial hardship.

What is resilience, by definition, is people's capacity to maintain a level head in the face of hardship. People with high resilience can deal with serious challenges like the ones analyzed by the researchers.

Various Definitions of Resilience

Despite the preceding description, what resilience means on a scientific level is a mixed bag. For a while, it was limited to a set of consistent individual characteristics. However, researchers were not quite convinced. The idea of resilience has evolved during the previous decade.

It evolved into an outcome and dynamic process based on interactions between individual and ambient elements.

Today, resilience is often defined as the process of successfully responding to adversity, trauma, tragedy, danger, or severe causes of stress. This description incorporates the "bounce-back" trait, which is one of the most important aspects of resilience.

The Value of Resilience

People are feeling overwhelmed and unable to handle the high expectations of their everyday life as a result of ever-increasing demands on their time and energy.

As a consequence, individuals are always multitasking, continu- ously distracted, and pushed in too many directions. If you want to remain at the top of your game in life and at business, you must understand how to skillfully navigate your way through difficult situations.

There are four more reasons why resilience is a valuable life skill.

1. Turn Failure Into Success

In my experience, the path to success is fraught with failure. It is a natural part of existence. Building resilience requires a willingness to fail.

Those who are unable to recover from hardship end up inter-nalizing failure and eventually quitting. If you identify with this style of thinking, it's critical to grasp that failure is an occurrence. It does not define your personality.

It was shown that when you attempt, fail, try again, and eventually succeed, your dopaminergic reward system gives you a pleasant kick. This is what gives you the necessary impetus when adversity strikes like a ton of bricks.

Failure is only a stepping stone that everyone encounters on their journey to greatness. You must ask yourself whether you are ready to take big chances to become the person you've always wanted to be.

2. Create an internal locus of control.

Do you think life occurs to you or for you? To increase your hap- piness in any aspect of your life, you must first ask yourself the challenging question, "Who is responsible for my happiness?"

Your response to this question will decide how well you can overcome obstacles in life.

People who have an external locus of control find it difficult to recover from life's shocks. They think that external influences dictate the course of their life. Not surprisingly, many feel helpless as a result of this thinking.

Resilient persons with an internal locus of control, on the other hand, perceive themselves as the CEO of their life. They understand that they have complete power over every choice they make.

They can bounce back after being knocked down, implying that they may utilize life's biggest obstacles as springboards for achievement. When you do this, you take control of your fate, and resilience becomes your natural condition.

3. Create Positive Beliefs

What does the term "resilience" imply to you? Asking that question reveals a lot about your beliefs. When your world crumbles around you, it's easy to become negative and play the "why me" game. However, you cannot conquer life's obstacles if you believe the Universe is not on your side. Negativity will get you nowhere in life.

The experience of managing pleasant emotions, even in the middle of a very challenging or stressful period, is a crucial aspect that leads to resilience.

A resilient individual overcomes obstacles by harnessing the power of good emotions and calling on their support network when required. They can reinterpret hardship into something beneficial, allowing them to recover and build long-term objec- tives.

4. Assists You in Accepting Change

A basic reality is at the core of resilience: change is unavoidable. We live in a world that is always changing. In reality, the only certainty we can rely on is ambiguity.

People make mistakes when they ignore or oppose change. As a consequence, since they are unable to find consolation in the turmoil, they end up living a life of agony and suffering.

You will not develop resilience by staying in your comfort zone.

Breaking loose from the bonds of security and diving into the unknown is the only way to fully develop and extend oneself.

This will need some intense inner work, such as adjusting limiting beliefs, overcoming harmful behaviors, and learning how to make friends with stress.

Let's be honest... Nobody like confronting their "stuff," yet it is a necessary step in becoming resilient.

Last Thoughts

When life throws you a curveball, believe that you are strong enough to continue in the game. Adversity may bend you, but it will never break you.

It is unimportant how many times you fall.. All that counts is that you get back up and go forth.

4

Chapter 4

Personal anecdotes illustrating the power of resilience

#1. Resilience Short Stories - From Olympic Dream to Paralympic Dream

Peter has been swimming since he was three years old. Since then, he has won several medals in swimming competitions. He was known as "Dolphin!" His ambition was to bring home an Olympic medal for his nation.

Peter and his father were in a vehicle one day, driving to a swimming event. Their automobile was involved in an accident while driving. He and his father were both seriously hurt.

They were sent to a neighboring hospital for treatment. Unfortunately, Peter's father died as a result of a terrible head injury in which he lost both hands.

It took him many days to become cognizant. Hearing that his father was no longer with him, as well as the agony of losing both of his hands, ruined his dream.

He returned home after three months of therapy. He was troubled by the emptiness left by his father's death.

As time passed, he stumbled upon an old poster made by his father that said, "Proud to be Peter's father." My kid will one day win an Olympic gold. He burst out laughing as soon as he saw this. When his mother heard this, she rushed over to soothe him.

"Peter, Your father has always encouraged you to excel in swimming, Peter," she remarked"

"How can I, Mom?" he answered. "Why can't you see me?"

"This is not the end of the world," she pointed out.. To find a means to make your goal a reality. My Dolphin, there is always a way."

Peter then began studying the road to realizing his ambition, with a medal at the Paralympics as his goal. It was initially tough for him throughout training. But he was tough, however, and he worked hard.

Peter began competing in para-swimming competitions. He gradually improved and continued to smash records. Then he began winning competitions. He was chosen to represent his nation in the Paralympics after two years of hard effort.

Peter competed and earned two gold medals and one silver medal for his nation, as well as two world records.

When he got home, he told his mother, "Mom, I fulfilled my father's dream." However, this is not the end!"

He went on to win many medals in the Paralympics.

The moral of the tale is:

Have faith that this is not the end of the world. Push yourself harder to recover from the adversity. Be resilient to recover and attain your goals.

It's simple for anybody to dwell on the past and withdraw from society. Remember that you can always come back. It will be difficult at first, but as the days pass, you will find yourself in a zone of resilience.

#2. Resilience Short Stories - The Fear of Public Speaking

inspirational moral tales about overcoming the fear of public speaking

Raghu had been a shy kid from infancy. He'd always been shy around people. After graduating high school, he enrolled in college, which required him to move to a place other than his hometown.

He remained in a college hostel for the first time in his life, away from his family. Staying with so many people around him was a new experience for him.

He felt at ease in his surroundings and began conversing freely with his classmates and professors. Raghu's confidence began to skyrocket. He began practicing public speaking with the assistance of his buddies.

He was given the chance to deliver a speech at the college's annual function one day. He had done an excellent job of preparing for the occasion.

He became worried on the day of the event because of the enormous audience. His body began to quiver, and he was unable to speak. Students started murmuring throughout the auditorium. Raghu's lecturer, seeing his difficulty, instructed him to present at the conclusion.

Raghu rushed backstage and began sobbing. "Raghu, you prepared very hard for this," his buddy consoled. Simply eliminate any ideas from your head. You are strong. Go ahead and offer yourself; I know you can do it."

He returned to the present after some time. He was still tense. He took a few long breaths and told himself, "You are tougher than you believe." You can do it."

His voice drew the attention of everyone in the audience as he began his speech. He was confident and quickly got into the groove.

Following his speech, he received a standing ovation from the audience. Raghu delivered one of the greatest talks that day.

The moral of the tale is:

Opportunities are few. Even if you miss them on the first try, you must recover fast and try again.

The more failures you endure, the more robust you become. And in the future, whenever you face adversity, you will be able to bounce back and achieve your achievement and happiness.

#3. Short Resilience Stories - Resilient Family

family resilience short tales

A family of four lived in a village. Father worked as a mechanic, and mother as a tailor. They were the parents of two girls. They intended to relocate to the city for their daughter's schooling.

Both of their girls were accepted into a well-known school. The father became a mechanic at a firm, while the mother became a tailor in a textile company.

The burden for both father and mother grew as the days went on. Some of their father's coworkers outsource much of their work to him since they wield the authority of being major members of the Employee's Union and him being a rookie and outsider. On the mother's side, her firm requires her to work extra to enhance productivity.

Meanwhile, children in their daughter's class began making fun of them. They expressed their displeasure to their parents. "Throughout everyday life, we might confront misfortune, and it might influence every one of us in an unexpected way," his dad said. But it is up to us to determine how we will respond to this.

As a result, I recommend that you respond favorably. Concentrate on your academics. You may complain to the professors if things get out of hand. Otherwise, concentrate on your life; others will soon understand."

Then his mom addressed him, "We're experiencing the same thing at work." "How would it be a good idea for us to respond?"
"Right now, we need to educate our daughters and improve our financial situation," he said. As a result, we must handle stress and utilize it as a stepping stone in our lives. To recover from harsh conditions, we must be resilient."

As the years passed, they all advanced in their careers. They were a happy and financially secure family.

The older daughter goes on to become a doctor, while the younger one goes on to become a pilot. Father is now the Union head and main mechanic. Mother is now a manager in her firm.

Throughout their lives, they faced difficulty, stress, dangers, health issues, and financial difficulties. But, as a family, they confronted each circumstance with resilient habits, attitudes, and actions that helped them develop and accomplish their goals.

The moral of the tale is:

Life is full of twists and turns, and it presents us with new problems every day. It has a distinct impact on every one of us. But if we are robust, we can handle them pleasantly.

We may learn to be resilient in a variety of ways. We may learn over time through experiencing difficult circumstances and rebounding. It gives you the ability to develop and better your life.

5

Chapter 5

Personal narratives have an amazing way of bringing resilience to life. They offer vivid illustrations of how people have over- come hardship, defied the odds, and succeeded in the face ofadversity. Letuslookatafewpersonalexamplesthat demonstrate people's everlasting strength and resilience:

Anecdote No. 1: The Phoenix Rising

Meet Sarah, a young lady who has suffered a string of calamitous misfortunes. She fell into a downward spiral of self-doubt and misery after losing her job. Sarah, on the other hand, chose to be resilient rather than submit to the weight of her circumstances. She sought assistance from her loved ones, reflected on herself, and devised a strategy to reinvent herself. She followed her passion and founded her own company with unflinching perse- verance. Sarah used her toughest circumstances as a catalyst for personal development, demonstrating that failures can be stepping stones to achievement.

Anecdote No. 2: From Tragedy to Victory

Consider John, a survivor of a horrible accident that immobilized him from the waist down. He was first overcome by sadness, resentment, and a feeling of powerlessness. However, as time went on, John realized he had an unbreakable spirit. He began on a road of recovery and self-discovery with the help of his family and friends. Despite the physical difficulties, John refused to let his surroundings define him. He engaged himself in adapted sports, inspiring others and accomplish- ing athletic achievements he previously thought unattainable. John's tale exemplifies the transformational power of resilience, demonstrating that even in the face of enormous tragedy, the human spirit can rise above and accomplish extraordinary accomplishments.

Anecdote 3: Finding Hope Amid Adversity

Meet Maria, a mother who has gone through the agony of losing her kid. Maria might have let her grief overwhelm her in the depths of despair. She converted her anguish into a force for change, though, because of her undying love for her kid. Maria committed herself to help other grieving parents by starting a support group where people may find comfort and understanding. Maria's perseverance transformed her tragedy into a spark for compassion and healing, reminding us that there is strength to be found even in the darkest of times.

These human experiences serve as reminders that resilience is a genuine and transformational power inside each of us, not just an abstract idea. They show that resilience is not limited to the exceptional few, but is available to everybody ready to tap into their inner power. We are motivated to believe in our ability to endure, develop, and prosper in the face of adversity by sharing these experiences.

These examples provide witness to the extraordinary power of resilience, illustrating that it is not the absence of obstacles that defines our life, but rather our capacity to overcome them. They encourage us to embrace our resilience, knowing that we have the strength to overcome, the bravery to continue, and the unflinching drive to construct a better future inside us.

6

Chapter 6

The role of mindset in overcoming challenges

When faced with difficulties and uncertainties, there are two options. Oneisbeingoverwhelmedbywhatisgoingonin the world. The second approach is to develop and maintain a successful attitude.

Two years of living with a pandemic has left us traumatized. Covid-19 was the first, followed by the Delta and Omicron varieties. There was a brief sense of relief between each wave that we were finally getting out of this morass. Unfortunately, every time it seemed like there was light at the end of the tunnel, it turned out to be another train heading straight for us.

Now we must be concerned about Russia's conflict in Ukraine

and the possibility of it involving the United States and other na- tions. Everyone is concerned about the potential of a desperate Putin detonating a nuclear weapon.

With all of this worry and anxiety, it's no surprise that mental health problems are at an all-time high. It's reasonable if you're worn out and want to quit. It's simple to curl up in bed, pull the covers over your head, and pray for the best—or you may take command of your life and work. This may be accomplished by cultivating a successful attitude. Making a habit of how you see and react to things is what a mentality is.

The majority of individuals have a fixed attitude. They accept themselves as they are and argue that they are unable to change. This does not have to be the case. You may discover how to create a successful attitude successfully. To begin, you may exert control over how you see the world around you, analyze events, and build a healthy, productive response.

Most individuals respond to circumstances instinctively and withoutconsideration. Ifsomeonesaysanythingharshor unpleasant to you, your natural response will be to feel horrible about yourself, let the insult spoil your day, and reinforce any sentiments of poor self-esteem. You may also react impulsively, exacerbating the situation.

We may detect attributes such as tenacity, drive, enthusiasm, and the capacity to fall, dust oneself off, and get back up by studying successful people. It is possible to regulate your thoughts. Instead of responding impulsively or acting out of habit, you may adjust the way you process events and then move in a constructive path.

It is possible to develop a successful attitude. Most individuals succumb to the negative voices in their heads that have been instilled in them from childhood. These never-ending cycles batter you with negativity, worry, failure, and uncertainty. It gets more convenient to do nothing.

To be successful, you must first identify your goals. Find a larger goal to drive you. Make a strategy to reach your objective. Use positive self-talk to be your salesperson. Begin focusing on regular routines that will better prepare you for success. Avoid negative haters by surrounding oneself with like-minded positive individuals. Improve your communication skills to seem more assured. Begin utilizing affirmations, mantras, and journaling to make your dreams a reality.

It is not a good idea to expect a change to happen on its own. Wanting, waiting, and longing will not provide results. To reach a goal, you must have a strong desire to succeed as well as the ability to act.

This is true for your work and career. It's easy to get insulted during an interview. Don't let it bother you. Ignore the slights and indignities. Instead, imagine yourself landing the job and receiving a large rise and bonus. Rise above the disrespect. Develop mental resilience as well as a good response to rejection. Use every "thank you, but we are going in a different direction for the job" as fuel to locate a job that is even better than the one you didn't get.

When it comes to interviews, write out all of your objectives and devise a strategy to attain them. Refresh your résumé and LinkedIn page to ensure it captures the attention of recruiters, hiring managers, and human resource experts. Be courageous and cold when reaching out to recruiters who specialize in your field. Start building a network of supporting individuals if you haven't already. This tribe will participate in activities that will benefit both parties. Practice your elevator pitch and do research on the hiring managers and individuals you will meet with throughout the interview process.

Push yourself to work on components of your interview success strategy every day. Maintain a consistent and concentrated approach to the program daily. Remind yourself of the reasons you're seeking a new career. It may be earning more money to better your family's life. You may wish to look for a better opportunity if you presently feel underappreciated or exploited. These steps will lead to your success in acquiring the position and income you want.

Consider your prior triumphs. Consider all of the instances you triumphed against hardship. Most individuals throw their triumphs about them like dust. This becomes a mountain. Do the opposite: gather all of your wonderful, positive, and winning experiences and construct them into a gigantic New York City office complex. When negative ideas arise, gaze at the shining structure to inspire you to pursue what may seem to be unattainable. What you desire will come true if you have a successful attitude.

7

Chapter 7

How To Have The Mindset To Overcome Challenges That Hold You Back

When it comes to conquering obstacles, having the appropriate mentality is critical.
 Whether we regard problems as insurmountable or as chances for progress is determined by our thinking.

Growth Mindset vs. Fixed Mindset

To begin, it's critical to grasp the distinction between a fixed mentality and a growth mindset. People with a fixed mentality feel that their talents and qualities are unchangeable.

26

Because they do not feel they can progress, they may shun difficulties and give up quickly. People with a growth mindset, on the other hand, feel that their talents and attributes can be developed through work and study.

Encourage yourself to look for ways to develop and improve.

Accepting Failure

Accepting failure is an important element of having a development mentality. Failure is often seen negatively, although it is an essential component of the learning process.

When we fail, we may learn from our errors and improve our performance the following time. Instead of being afraid of failure, we should embrace it as a tremendous learning opportunity.

A growth mentality is characterized by a positive attitude.

A good attitude is another crucial part of having a development mindset.

We are more likely to discover answers and conquer obstacles when we approach them with a positive mindset.

Negative attitudes and self-doubt may stifle our progress and make it harder to identify chances for advancement. We may open ourselves up to fresh options and possible solutions by concentrating on the good.

Having a development mentality necessitates self-awareness.

Aside from having a happy mindset, it's also important to be self-aware.

Knowing our strengths and shortcomings might help us find areas for improvement and concentrate our efforts.

Being conscious of our thoughts and emotions may also help us regulate them more efficiently.

Having a growth mentality necessitates constant progress.

It is also necessary to have a growth attitude while studying to create a growth mindset. This requires a desire to learn as well as an openness to new ideas and opinions.

It also entails being willing to invest the time and effort required to learn new things, even if they are challenging. We may con- tinue to develop and improve throughout our lives if we regard learning as a lifetime process rather than simply something we do in school.

A development mentality entails having a feeling of purpose.

Finally, having a development mentality implies a feeling of purpose.

We are more likely to remain motivated and focused on our objectives when we have a feeling of purpose. This may assist us in overcoming obstacles and achieving success.

Having a development mentality is critical for conquering obsta- cles.

To summarize, having a growth mentality is critical for conquering obstacles that hold us back.

We may create the mentality we need to overcome difficulties and accomplish our objectives by accepting failure, having a good attitude, being self-aware, having a growth mindset in learning, and having a sense of purpose.

It's vital to remember that cultivating a development mindset is a lifelong process that needs work and dedication. However, by keeping these ideas in mind, we may equip ourselves with the skills we need to reach our maximum potential.

8

Chapter 8

Investigating the Growth mentality

Peterson park, a famous psychologist, pioneered the notion of a growth mindset, which has transformed our understanding of human development and resilience. The concept that our talents and intellect can be grown and improved through commitment, effort, and a desire to learn is at the heart of a growth mindset. Let us now investigate the development mindset and its transforming power:

The Influence of Belief :

The concept that our perceptions about our skills impact our capacity for progress is central to the growth mindset. Adopting a growth mindset entails accepting that intellect and skill are flexible attributes that can be developed through time. We open up a world of possibilities and begin on a path of continual development when we believe in our ability to progress.

Accepting Difficulties:

Individuals who have a development mentality see barriers as opportunities for progress rather than hurdles to be avoided. Instead of avoiding challenging jobs, they see them as opportu- nities to learn, acquire new talents, and broaden their capacities. Taking on difficulties with zeal and perseverance encourages people to stretch themselves beyond their comfort zones, over- come disappointments, and eventually achieve greater success.

Putting Effort and Persistence First:

A development mentality emphasizes hard work and perse- verance. Individuals with this attitude realize the importance of hard effort, practice, and devotion to achievement. They understand that setbacks and mistakes are a natural part of the learning process and see them as stepping stones toward success. Instead of getting disheartened by failures, they keep a resilient mentality and utilize setbacks to enhance their tactics and approach.

Developing a Passion for Learning:

Those with a growth mindset value the process of learning much. They tackle new difficulties with curiosity, hoping to learn new things and talents. They understand that learning is a lifetime process and are receptive to feedback, constructive criticism, and self-improvement. Individuals with a growth mindset embrace personal growth and development as a rewarding and continuing quest by cultivating a passion for learning.

Overcoming Difficulties:

Individuals with a development mentality see difficulties and disappointments as transitory setbacks rather than permanent constraints. Rather than being discouraged by failures, they see them as chances for problem-solving and innovative thinking. They are tenacious in seeking alternate tactics, learning from their failures, and adapting their ways to overcome obstacles. Individuals with this perspective may manage hurdles with perseverance, eventually leading to greater achievement.

Motivating Others:

One of the most appealing qualities of the development mentality is its ability to spread. People who have a development mentality are sources of inspiration and encouragement to people around them. They inspire learning, cooperation, and personal development by demonstrating a belief in growth and actively supporting others' attempts to enhance their strengths.

Exploring and embracing a development mindset has the potential to change our lives. It frees us from self-imposed constraints, feeds our desire for advancement, and provides us with the resilience to face life's obstacles. We engage on a road of personal development by accepting difficulties, persevering through failures, and constantly extending our horizons by knowing that our skills are not fixed but can be cultivated and enhanced. The growth mentality allows us to maximize our potential and uncover the limitless possibilities that await us.

9

Chapter 9

Methods for Developing a resilient attitude

Developing a more resilient attitude is critical for personal development and success. It may help you remain motivated, accomplish your objectives, and perhaps find more pleasure in your life.

We may open ourselves up to new options and build the lifestyles we desire by adopting healthier mental habits and attitudes.

1. Recognize and confront negative ideas

To develop a more optimistic attitude, you must detect negative ideas and counteract them with more positive thinking. This is examining why you are experiencing negative ideas and figuring out how to transform them into something more positive.

For example, if you believe you can't accomplish something, attempt to find proof that shows you are incorrect. This will assist you in staying focused on the positive and strong elements of yourself.

2. Show Gratitude and Appreciation
Gratitude may help us feel better and achieve our goals. Think about something you are grateful for every day to cultivate gratitude. Thank individuals for what they do for you, and compliment others.

Find the positive in any circumstance and appreciate everything excellent in your life. This will not only make you feel better, but it will also help you create healthier relationships and deeper connections.

3. Take some time to unwind and recharge.
You must take care of yourself to have a healthier attitude. Take time out of your day to rest and replenish your batteries. This might range from meditating to reading a book to taking a break to do something you like.

Find stress-relieving activities such as deep breathing techniques or yoga stretches. Taking frequent pauses can help you recover your body and mind, allowing you to think optimistically.

4. Create a strategy and set goals for yourself.

Setting objectives is essential for success and cultivating a good mentality. Set realistic objectives that are executable and quantifiable so that you can measure your progress. It's also critical to ensure that your objectives are something you want to achieve.

Writing out your objectives and devising a strategy to reach them will help you stay on track. And it's crucial to rejoice when you achieve one of these objectives because it will help push you for the next one.

5. Establish a good social network

Being around positive individuals might help you remain motivated and inspired to achieve your objectives. Make sure the people in your life are encouraging and supporting you so that they can aid you when things become rough.

Find a strong network of friends, family members, or mentors who will both challenge and encourage you. Having a good social network like this may be quite beneficial in building a positive outlook.

6. Look for Ways to Stay Motivated

It might be challenging to stay motivated and on track at times. To remain motivated, we must continuously remind ourselves of why we are doing something and what our ultimate aim is.

Reward yourself for tiny victories along the road to increase your motivation to keep going.

Make reminders to check in with your objectives and create a pleasant atmosphere where you may remain focused and inspired.

7. Instead of dwelling on mistakes, learn from them.
Making errors is a natural part of life, and we must learn from them rather than linger on them. Accept what you can't alter and concentrate on what you can do to go ahead.

Look for possibilities that arise from errors and utilize them to develop and learn from your experiences.

This will not only help you develop a healthier mentality, but it may also provide you with a chance to become more resilient and successful in the future.

8. Maintain Your Physical Health With Diet, Exercise, And Sleep
When it comes to creating a positive mentality, physical health is equally as vital as mental wellness. Eating good meals, exercising regularly, and getting enough sleep are all important for sustaining both mental and physical health.

Make careful to strike a balance between work and leisure time so that you may rest and replenish your body.

9. Foster a Resilient Attitude
The capacity to recover from hardship is referred to as resilience. A resilient mentality enables you to face life's obstacles with grace and resolve.

Accept failures as learning opportunities and devise tactics to overcome them. Remember that the goal is not to escape failure, but to learn from it and use it as a stepping stone to success.

10. Accept Failure as a Learning Experience

Failure is not the end, but rather a stepping stone to achievement. Accept failure as a normal part of the learning process and a chance to progress. Analyze your failures, learn from them, and apply what you've learned to future initiatives.

Reframing failure as feedback can help you develop resilience and a mentality that embraces difficulties.

Final Thoughts

Developing a more positive outlook is a continuous process that needs consistent work. However, by using these tactics, you may begin to transform your mindset toward more optimistic thinking.

Remember that mentality is something that must be worked on every day, not something that develops suddenly.

You can design the life you choose for yourself, so don't be afraid to take the first step.

10

Chapter 10

Understanding the nature of adversity

Adversity is unavoidable in life. It refers to the problems, obstacles, and setbacks that we confront in all aspects of our life, including personal, professional, and social. Adversity may manifest itself in a variety of ways, including financial troubles, health challenges, marital problems, job loss, and other unforeseen occurrences that disturb our daily routine. Adversity, on the other hand, is not necessarily negative. It may also be a source of personal development, learning, and progress.

Adversity has a complicated and multidimensional character. Depending on the context and individual experiences, it may be seen from several angles. Examining the effect of adversity on people and their reactions to it is one method to comprehend its nature. Adversity may have an impact on people's lives in both good and bad ways.

Adversity, on the other side, maybe a cause of tension, worry, and emotional distress. It has the potential to question our sense of identity, purpose, and meaning in life. Adversity may also cause physical and mental health issues including depression, anxiety disorders, and chronic stress. Adversity may also lead to social isolation, loneliness, and a feeling of separation from others.

11

Chapter 11

Human Nature and Resilience

What if you knew you'd come out of a challenging situation stronger, smarter, and even more resilient than before? How would you feel knowing that the choices you make the moment you become aware of a potential calamity would be correct?

When danger threatens, a leader's task and obligation is to assess the situation and then deliver reliable, up-to-date, and accurate information. People will also look to their leaders for compassion and a path ahead. There are five paths for discovering and replenishing your store of resilience when you need it the most. The approach is founded on a metaphor that reminds us that we are part of nature and are profoundly connected to its five elements: Earth, Water, Air, Fire, and

Ether. These components were previously regarded to be the foundation of everything. To be sure, our knowledge of the cosmos has become more intricate and sophisticated, but these aspects have remained constant, are a part of who we are, and have a message for us about human perseverance.

Resilience is characterized by the American Mental Affiliation ("APA") as "the most common way of adjusting great despite misfortune, injury, misfortune, dangers, or critical wellsprings of stress; it includes; it involves "bouncing back" and personal growth from experiences." Resilience may be built, leading to improved quality of life, increased attention, calm under pressure, improved memory, and more meaningful leadership. You have an option. With experience, you may build deeper resilience and emerge as the morale-boosting, competent leader you want and need to be, or you can succumb to the suffering, to your fear of making errors, and to the hope that the issues will just disappear.

There will be suffering.

There will be pain and suffering if you are living. Resilience will not protect you from pain, but it will lessen the severity and length of your suffering. In reality, it is hard to properly understand your resilience until you are given the "opportunity" to battle and suffer for your principles or your own (or the organization's) existence. Peril lurks around every corner; are you prepared? Consider the five attitudes listed below to help you handle upheaval and create resilience.

Get Grounded on Earth

To bend with or stay steadfast in the face of danger and un-certainty, you must be grounded. "Each unnerving occasion, regardless of how pessimistic it might show up from an external perspective, can possibly be horrible or not to the individual encountering it." The experience isn't built into the event." It is determined by how each individual sees and interprets its influence.

Consider a German Shepherd barking and charging at two persons, one of which is a dog lover and the other who is not an 'animal person.' Given that not every individual (leader or team) would sense danger from the same challenge, there must be a choice after the stimulus and before the reaction. The moment may be short, but there is flexibility to react in that microsecond. You may not be able to pick your initial response, but you can learn to de-escalate, become aware of potential alternatives, and make an intentional decision about what to do next. The resilient individual will pick their part to play as well as their attitude about what is occurring. Better judgments are made when self-awareness and situational awareness replace impulsivity or habit. When you are rooted in your beliefs and talents, you can boldly open your mind to consider choices, possibilities, and the perspectives of others.

Take note of your discomfort, then stop; identify your sensa-tions if possible. What are you concentrating on? What are your thoughts on the challenge? What if your assumptions are incorrect? Your considerations and ends without giving it much thought are not generally your best, so the sooner you perceive and refocus, the sooner you can return your concentration to the present and conclude what you have some control over, what to do straightaways to the present and decide what you can control, what to do next, and which aspects of the situation will require more time or information before acting.

As the pull of gravity consistently keeps us fast to Earth, so will the force of our experiences and quieted intuition lead us in our evaluations of what is occurring today and how it impacts ourselves, our teams, our organizations, the stakeholders, and the vision established to guide us.

Breathe to Reclaim Your Mind

When a challenge seems to be a danger, the activated brain responds with the fight, flight, or freeze reaction. There is no time to contemplate in such a situation, respiration becomes shallow, the heart rate increases and the entire concentration is on survival. Most of the time, our lives are not in danger, and it would be more beneficial to everyone involved if we could regain our brains and heart to confront the threat energetically and with calm, clear, strategic thinking.

Mindfulness improves performance, memory, and attention, promotes originality, and increases likeability. You may reduce your pulse rate and spark your capacity to reason, observe, and react consciously to what is both new and present at any moment by bringing your attention to your breath, slowing it down, and inhaling and exhaling more deeply. There's a reason airlines tell caregivers to put on their oxygen masks before assisting others. It's all about intentionally focusing on breathing in and out fresh air before performing. You're halfway there if you're already breathing:

"Pay close attention to your breathing. Don't attempt to control it; just notice the whole breath in and out. If you catch your mind wandering, just return it to your breathing and begin again with the next breath. Don't condemn yourself for having stray thoughts; we all do...the process of returning the attention to the breath seems to build the brain's wiring for concentration."

Our breathing is steady, centering, and restorative when we remain calm amid adversity. There is enough oxygen for us to share, so take as many centering breaths as you need until you acquire perspective on whether your life is in danger or whether your leadership is needed. If your life is in danger, flee! If you are called upon to lead, take a deep breath, center yourself, and determine what to do next.

Water: Ride the Wave to the Beach

Feeling overwhelmed and drowning in everyone else's cares and needs? Your life jacket assures that there will be a path through, under, over, or around the disruption. Your resilience will offer the buoyancy you need to persevere through difficult circumstances. Resilient leaders navigate, invent, and discover what may be useful along the route by using both their logical mind and their intuitive heart. The planet is 71% water, while the brain and heart are both 73% water. The human body is designed to ride and endure disruption waves.

I hit it, but it was unharmed. I whacked it again with all my power, but it remained unharmed! I then attempted to grab a hold of it, but it was impossible. This water, the softest material on the planet, enclosed in the tiniest container, simply seemed feeble. In truth, it might pierce the world's toughest material. That was the end of it! I aspired to be like water's natural state.

Leaders who get grounded, breathe, and then tackle issues with a calm, clear, inquiring, and caring brain and heart will always find a solution. Those that rely on you during tough times tend to defer and believe that their leader will fulfill the shared objective and ensure the survival of the greatest number of people feasible. Put on your oxygen mask first, then surf the waves to shore.

Capture and Apply the Heat of the Moment

Johnson shares his account of getting scorched on every inch of his body as a nine-year-old. He came close to death, spent 13 months in recuperation, lost his fingers, and now lives with scars. He was questioned whether he would do it again if given the chance. He said, "Yes." He discovered his calling through suffering, rebounding, maturing, and emerging stronger. He went on to work as a hospital chaplain, novelist, and motivational speaker.

A resilient leader develops the capacity to capitalize on the emotional strength that underpins our will to survive and prosper. According to John O'Leary, the distinction between being a victim and a victor is based on one question: "Why me?"

The victim of adversity is worn down by difficulty, burdened by sorrow and despair, and wonders, "Why me?" Why do I have to fight? What exactly did I do to deserve this? This is impossible for me. In contrast, Victor views adversity as an opportunity and wonders, "Why me?" What lessons may be drawn from this situation? How can I make this experience beneficial to myself and my team? This is occurring for a purpose; what am I being asked to do? Leaders who learn to observe, halt, become grounded, breathe, and manage their emotions amid a high-stakes situation may tap into that urge to survive and flow effectively through the hardship while motivating others to participate. Adversity, for resilient leaders, is a call to action to contribute what only they can give at that time in their lives.

What Is the Truth About Ether?

What if you understood why something bad was occurring, what to do, how everything ties together, and how everything would end? Ether is the element that fills up the gaps. The "primary focus" of deep listening is to listen below the surface of the discourse. Listen for the undercurrents and be interested in what's going on under the surface at the emotional and (team) dynamic levels'.

How does everything come together? Ether is the element that calls us to merge our cognitive and intuitive minds. This integration allows resilient leaders to see the larger picture while strategizing, communicating, acting decisively, and empower- ing others. Resilient leaders believe they are where they are intended to be and have what it takes to confront and overcome adversity. The educated 'gut' of resilient leaders educates them about what is occurring, what is likely to emerge next, and how to show up. They set aside their egos to view the greater picture and the role they are being asked to perform.

This is described as "putting oneself on the balcony" by Heifetz and Linsky to prevent becoming so caught up in the activity that you can only react. According to Goleman, "the ability to maintain perspective amid action" allows one to inquire and analyze "what is going on here?" There are three levels of consciousness: self-awareness, awareness of others, and awareness of the larger world.

Every leader must nurture this trio of awareness in plenty and the appropriate balance because failing to concentrate within leaves you rudderless, failing to focus on others leaves you ignorant, and failing to look outward leaves you blindsided.

Nobody knows who will be resilient or what the future contains, but people may tap into their inner five elements — Earth, Air, Water, Fire, and Ether – since they are part of our human nature. Practicing the five views amid adversity increases the likelihood that leaders and their teams will emerge stronger, smarter, and better equipped for the next, unavoidable crisis.

Cultivating self-compassion and self-esteem

When we face a setback at work, we either get defensive and blame others, or we criticize ourselves. Neither reaction is beneficial. Shielding responsibility by going on the defensive may take the sting out of failing, but it comes at the sacrifice of learning. Self-flagellation, on the other hand, may seem justified at the time, but it may lead to an incorrectly pessimistic estimate of one's potential, undermining personal growth.

Instead, we should be kind to ourselves. People who do this exhibit three characteristics: first, they are kind rather than judgmental about their failures and mistakes; second, they recognize that failures are a common human experience; and third, they take a balanced approach to negative emotions when they stumble or fall short—they allow themselves to feel bad, but they do not allow negative emotions to take over.

Self-compassion improves performance through instilling the "growth mindset"—the notion that progress is possible with commitment and hard effort. It also allows us to connect with our more real selves.

When individuals face a setback at work, whether it's a poor sales quarter, getting passed over for a promotion, or an inter-personal issue with a coworker, they often react in one of two ways. We either go on the defensive and blame others, or we scold ourselves. Unfortunately, neither answer is really useful. Shielding responsibility by going on the defensive may take the sting out of failing, but it comes at the sacrifice of learning. Self- flagellation, on the other hand, may seem justified at the time, but it may lead to an incorrectly pessimistic estimate of one's potential, undermining personal growth.

What if we instead treated ourselves as we would a buddy in a comparable situation? We'd probably be friendly, understanding, and encouraging. Self-compassion is the term for directing that sort of reaction inside, toward oneself, and it has received a lot of attention in recent years. Self-compassion is being discovered by psychologists to be a beneficial technique for improving performance in a range of situations, from healthy aging to sports. I and other scholars have started to concentrate on how self-compassion improves professional development.

Self-compassion is a less common notion to nonacademics than self-esteem or self-confidence. Although those who practice self-compassion have better self-esteem, the two notions are separate. Self-esteemisoftenassociatedwithcomparing oneself to others. Self-compassion, on the other hand, does not require criticizing oneself or one's surroundings. Instead, it fosters self-esteem by encouraging individuals to care about their well-being and rehabilitation following a setback.

People who have a high level of self-compassion exhibit three behaviors: first, they are kind rather than judgmental about their failures and mistakes; second, they recognize that failures are a common human experience; and third, they take a balanced approach to negative emotions when they stumble or fall short—they allow themselves to feel bad, but they don't let negative emotions take over.

A professor has created a questionnaire that measures the three components of self-compassion. Researchers and practitioners have used the tool to shed light on what personality traits and behaviors are associated with self-compassion, discovering, for example, that people who score high typically have greater motivation to improve themselves and are more likely to report strong feelings of authenticity—the sense of being true to oneself. Both are critical components of a successful career. The good news is that each of these characteristics may be developed and improved via self-compassion.

A Growth Attitude

Most companies and individuals desire to develop, and self-compassion is essential for this. We commonly equate personal development with tenacity, dedication, and hard effort, yet the process often begins with introspection. One of the most important prerequisites for self-improvement is a truthful evaluation of where we stand—of our strengths and limits. Convincing ourselves that we are better than we are led to complacency while believing we are worse leads to defeatism. People who treat themselves with compassion are better able to come to accurate self-assessments, which is the basis for progress. They are also more driven to improve their flaws rather than asking themselves, "What's the point?" and to summon the tenacity necessary to improve abilities and break bad habits.

People who practice self-compassion are more likely to adopt a development mentality.

My colleagues and I established this in a series of trials in which individuals were encouraged to treat themselves with either compassion or self-esteem. Then we rated their motivation to develop themselves. In one research, we asked individuals to recount a moment when they did something they believed was wrong and felt guilt, remorse, and regret as a consequence. The bulk of individuals' sins concerned romantic adultery, academic misconduct, dishonesty, violation of trust, or injuring someone close to them. The participants were then randomized at random to one of three conditions: self-compassion, self- esteem, or a control group. Participants in self-compassion were instructed to write a paragraph to themselves showing kindness and understanding about the transgression. People with low self-esteem were asked to compose a paragraph out- lining their good attributes. Control group participants were instructed to write about an activity they loved. Following that, all participants completed a questionnaire measuring their intention to make apologies and their determination to not repeat the mistake in the future. Participants who were urged to treat themselves with compassion were more motivated to make apologies and never repeat the transgression than those who were encouraged to react to the transgression in a self-esteem- boosting way or those in the control group. In another study, we discovered that self-compassion enhanced the determination of persons who believed they were responsible for a romantic breakup to be better partners in future relationships when compared to participants in the other two circumstances.

Self-compassion does more than only assist individuals in overcoming failure or setbacks. It also supports what Stanford University psychology professor Carol Dweck refers to as a "growth mindset." Dweck has shown the advantages of adopting a "growth" rather than "fixed" approach to performance, whether it is in starting a successful start-up, parenting, or running a marathon. People with a fixed mentality believe that personality characteristics and talents, including their own, are fixed. They feel that who we are now is fundamentally who we will be in five years. People with a development mindset, on the other hand, see personality characteristics and talents as flexible. They recognize the opportunity for improvement and are therefore more inclined to attempt to improve—to put in the work and practice, as well as to remain cheerful and hopeful.

According to my findings, self-compassion causes individuals to adopt a development mentality. In one research I did, participants were asked to name their largest weakness—most of which concerned social challenges such as lack of confidence, anxiety, shyness, and relationship insecurity—before being randomly allocated to one of three groups. "Imagine you are talking to yourself about this weakness from a compassion- ate and understanding perspective," participants in the self- compassion group were encouraged to write. What are your thoughts?"People in the self-esteem group were asked to write in response to: "Imagine that you are talking to yourself about this shortcoming from the standpoint of affirming your good (rather than negative) attributes." The last group was not asked to write anything.

Following that, participants completed a series of assessments to determine whether they were satisfied, sad, or disturbed and were then asked to spend five minutes expressing if they'd ever done anything to alter their weakness and where they believed their weakness originated. Independent coders scored partici- pants' replies depending on whether they had a growth or fixed attitude ("It's just inborn—there's nothing I can do" vs "With hard work, I know I can change"). The self-compassion condition participants indicated considerably more ideas connected with a development attitude than the other two conditions.

However, what about real behavior? How can we be certain that self-compassion, and the accompanying development attitude, will motivate individuals to try harder to better themselves? One of the most persuasive evidence that a person has a growth mindset, according to the scientific literature on fixed and growth mindsets, is his or her propensity to keep striving to do better despite getting unfavorable feedback. After all, there's no use in putting in the effort if you assume your talents are fixed. However, if you consider your talents to be malleable, receiving unfavorable comments should not prevent you from striving to develop.

We put this logic to the test in a research in which participants (all students at a highly rated institution) initially completed an extremely tough vocabulary exam and were told they did badly. Theparticipantswerethendividedintotwogroups at random. "If you had difficulty with the test you just took, you're not alone," the researcher said to the first group, the self-compassion condition. It is normal for pupils to struggle with assessments like these. If you're unhappy with how you performed, don't be too harsh on yourself." To the other set of participants, the researcher added, "If you had problems with the exam you just completed, don't feel awful about yourself— you must be brilliant if you got into this institution."

Following that, everyone was informed they had to take another vocabulary exam. They were allowed to study a list of terms and meanings and were told that they may go over the words as many times as they wished before taking the exam. We discovered that individuals who were encouraged to see their first failure with compassion were more likely to adopt a development perspective regarding their language skills and spend more time learning than their self-esteem peers. Self-compassion seems to have opened the way for self-development by rekindling their desire to do better, fostering the notion that progress is attainable, and inspiring people to try harder.

Being Self-Reliant

Beyond improving workers' motivation to develop, self-compassion provides workplace advantages. It may help individuals gravitate toward jobs that better match their personalities and beliefs over time. Living by one's actual self —what psychologists refer to as "authenticity"—increases motivation and drive (along with a slew of other mental health advantages). Unfortunately, many people in the workplace struggle to be real. People may feel trapped in positions where they must repress their actual selves due to incongruent workplace rules about conduct, misgivings about what they can offer, or anxieties of being assessed adversely by coworkers and superiors. However, self-compassion may assist individuals in assessing their career and personal trajectories and making appropriate course changes. A self-compassionate sales executive who misses a quarterly goal, for example, will not only consider how she can make her numbers the next quarter, but she will also consider if she is in the correct kind of career for her temperament and disposition.

We noticed that cultivating self-compassion fosters authenticity by reducing negative thoughts and self-doubts. In the first trial, participants completed a brief survey every day for one week. Ev- ery day, they were asked to score their self-compassion ("Today, I showed caring, understanding, and kindness toward myself") and authenticity ("Today, I felt authentic and genuine in my interactions with others"). We discovered that daily fluctuations in self-compassion levels were strongly related to variations in sentiments of authenticity. On days when participants reported being more sympathetic toward themselves than usual, they also reported higher levels of authenticity.

These correlational results were supported by experimental data from another research in which individuals were randomly allocated to react to a personal vulnerability from a self- compassionate, self-esteem-boosting, or neither viewpoint. They immediately completed surveys to determine how genuine they felt. Participants who were told to be self-compassionate about their flaws reported much greater levels of authenticity than those in the other two situations.

Self-compassion may assist individuals in gravitating to jobs that are more suited to their nature.

What's going on here? Treating oneself with love, understanding, and without judgment reduces anxiety about social rejection, clearing the path for authenticity. Optimism seems to have a role as well. People who have an optimistic view of life are more prepared to take risks, such as expressing their actual selves. Indeed, optimistic individuals are more inclined to divulge unpleasant aspects of themselves, such as upsetting experiences or significant medical issues. As a result, optimism boosts people's willingness to be real, regardless of the dangers associated. I feel that the emotional serenity and balanced viewpoint that comes with self-compassion may help individuals face challenging events with optimism.

Leadership that has been turbocharged

A sympathetic attitude toward oneself provides advantages that extend to others. This is particularly true for those in positions of authority. This is because self-compassion and compassion for others are inextricably linked: practicing one strengthens the other. Being kind and nonjudgmental toward oneself is good practice for treating others compassionately, just as compassion for others can increase one's compassion for oneself, creating an upward cycle of compassion—and an antidote to the "incivility spirals" that all too often plague workplaces.

The idea that self-compassion promotes a development men-tality is equally significant in this context. When leaders adopt a growth mindset (believing that change is possible), they are more likely to notice changes in subordinates' perfor- mance and provide meaningful comments on how to improve. Subordinates, in turn, may detect growth mindsets in their bosses, which makes them more motivated and happy, as well as more inclined to adopt growth mindsets themselves. The proverb "lead by example" relates to self-compassion and the development mentality that it fosters.

For authenticity, there is a comparable bond between leader and subordinate. People can detect authenticity in others, and when leaders are seen to be true to themselves, an aura of authenticity pervades the workplace. There is also abundant evidence that when individuals feel real in their interactions with others, they form better connections.

Leaders gain when they react to mistakes and setbacks with self- compassion. They are more likely to demonstrate psychological and behavioral characteristics that auger well for their profes- sional growth and success. And the advantages may flow down to subordinates, making self-compassion a win-win situation for both leaders and those they lead.

Developing Self-Compassion

It is not tough to cultivate self-compassion. It is a skill that can be learned and improved upon. I recommend adopting psychologists' notion of self-compassion as a three-point checklist for the analytically inclined: Am I being kind and understanding to myself? Do I accept flaws and failures as universal human experiences? Am I keeping my negative emotions in check? If this doesn't work, try a simple "trick": write yourself a letter in the third person, as if you were a friend or loved one. Many of us are better at being good friends to others than we are at being good friends to ourselves, which might help us avoid cycles of defensiveness or self-flagellation.

In recent years, the business world as a whole has done an excellent job of reducing the stigma associated with failure at the organizational level—it's a natural outcome of experimenting and, eventually, invention. However, far too many of us are fail- ing to see the restorative value of failure in our own professional life. This talent will grow increasingly vital as more sectors are disrupted and people's work lives are upended.

Don't berate yourself if you're having difficulty cultivating self- compassion in your work and personal life. You can improve with some practice.

12

Chapter 12

Shifting perspectives in difficult situations

The capacity to observe a problem from numerous angles seems to be an uncommon skill these days. We, humans, create tunnel vision anytime we are personally touched by a place, scenario, statement, or action. We make fast judgments and judgments based on how we initially see the whole scenario and find it difficult to change that first assessment.

Changing your attitude may help you solve the most difficult problems in life.

I'm not dismissing this characteristic. It's what kept our forefathers alive on the savanna: when a predator was detected and the impulse to flee kicked in, we survived to live another day and perhaps pass on our lion-dodging DNA to the next generation.

The problem is that humans no longer live on the savanna, and avoiding lions isn't something most people do regularly. We're far more inclined to avoid a colleague because of anything said at last year's Christmas party. Or a buddy we've been attempting to meet who appears to be avoiding us for inexplicable reasons. Or that barista at our favorite coffee shop who always seems... surely.

And don't even get me started on the man in the Tahoe who cut me off the other day. Jerk.

I have a personality characteristic that causes me to observe interpersonal events from numerous angles at once. I've educated myself to separate them so I can evaluate each one separately; formerly, I was a hot mess if a colleague brought up a controversial issue, a student launched an in-class argument, or even when that nasty barista attempted to murder me with eye daggers.

Trust me, it's not as awesome as it sounds.

So, what am I getting at, and why am I expressing what looks to be a personal rant? Shifting views is a useful technique to have in your arsenal. It might help you clarify your alternatives and decide which path to go with that large job. It may also assist you in navigating a hostile colleague scenario. The capacity to take a step back and examine a problem from many perspectives is fantastic.

Everything depends on your point of view.

But first, some context. I came across an intriguing essay on Placemakers a while back that provided a wonderful, concise history of the NIMBY (Not In My Back Yard) movement. The author's purpose was to highlight where the movement took a turn for the...let's say, worse, and it contains what I believe to be a vital life lesson regarding perspective:

"It is now your responsibility to cease telling them what you don't want. And begin telling them what you desire."

In other words, if you spend your entire focus on the terrible, you will most likely miss all of the great. This seems especially topical considering the nature of the 24/7 news cycle and most people's fixation with discussing it over the water cooler—both metaphorical and literal. Don't get so preoccupied with a bad, say, news report that you miss out on all the great things that are occurring all around you, frequently right under your nose. And, whatever you do, don't be scared to bring them up during such conversations. You may be amazed at how many other individuals will leap at the chance to speak about something NON-sensational.

Take a step back and look at these instances as learning op-portunities if you can't escape unfavorable discourse about a job endeavor, for example. Instead of saying, "You can't do ABC," say, "I wonder if XYZ would work?" You may be surprised that by reframing the problem in this way, you can achieve achievements you'll be pleased with. Not to mention obtaining the backing of the team members who first proposed ABC. By NOT dismissing their concept, but rather suggesting an alternative, you demonstrate to them that you do value their thoughts, if maybe not in this circumstance.

Perspective Change Produces Results

Results that bring you what you want rather than merely not getting what you don't want.

Don't believe NIMBYism is limited to where people live; it may be found in the workplace as well. If not multiples of one.

NIMBYs devote so much of their time and energy to opposing things they don't want - bridges, trails, airport runways (to name a few examples from Seattle) - that they frequently overlook what they already have - community. These same individuals lose out on the same feeling of community—called team cohesiveness in this case—at work because they are so focused on opposing proposals that threaten their control or project ideas that reduce them to a lower position than they believe they deserve.

What if these groups of neighbors came together more often than only when there was a hearing and chose to construct a community garden on a vacant property instead? Or banded together to assist an elderly neighbor in repairing their home so they could continue to live independently - and stay a part of their community? And what if those coworkers took a moment to listen to the thoughts of their colleagues? What if they took the time to look at the project through the eyes of someone else? Could they grasp that, although their function is little, their influence would be felt considerably more strongly when they are released?

Frank is a movement expert I first encountered while preparing for my personal trainer certification (yes, I come from a diverse background). On the surface, his concepts seem to be straight- forward. Simplyflippingyourviewpointonanything180 degrees gives you a whole other perspective. You could discover that you can see things from someone else's perspective, making it simpler to reach an agreement.

So, why is it so damn difficult most of the time?

For starters, there's something known as [The Backfire Effect]. This theory, at its most basic, states that no matter how much 'fact' you throw at someone, at best they will not change their deeply held view at all - and at worst, you will instead enhance this conviction. So your prospects of convincing this individual to see things your way' are slim.

In terms of what Frank is referring to above, our Western medi- cal system is the embodiment of a deeply ingrained mentality that states, 'cure the symptom.' It says nothing regarding the cause. If you come in with a stuffy nose, you'll be given a decongestant to help dry up the mucus in your sinuses. If you have a fever, you will be given medication to reduce your temperature. Never mind that mucus and fever are your body's natural defenses, how it protects itself against an invader. By treating the symptom, you never get to the stage of determining what your body is attempting to defend itself against, and you essentially shut off your defenses before they have a chance to begin working.

To return to our subject of workplace politics and toxic colleagues, if you can perceive a disagreement problem through the eyes of that toxic coworker, you may just be able to locate the fundamental reason to address it. Arguing and attempting to impose your point of view on them will result in disaster (if you don't believe me, consider the past X times you attempted it that way). So the objective is to be the person in this dispute who takes a step back, loops around, and looks at the problem from the other side of the room. That fever might be triggered by a workflow item stuck in another team's queue.

The health comparison and the job condition have one thing in common: your objective is to uncover the main problem and cure it rather than treating the symptoms with bandages.

To Truly See It, Get It Out of Your Head.

Among the several backgrounds I mentioned, I received a Graduate Certificate in Coaching a few years ago. Along with a very fun year-long learning experience, I walked away with a toolkit of coaching strategies that I have used as I transitioned from the IT industry to freelancing. A visualization approach I use almost every day is perhaps the single most significant item in that package, the one that helped me gain a grasp on the multiple-perspectives personality feature I mentioned earlier.

The concept is straightforward: to perceive a topic or event from numerous perspectives, you must first remove it from your brain.

Stop
Close your eyes for a moment.
   Take five deep, deliberate breaths (in for a count of four, hold for a count of four, out for a count of six).
        Consider the circumstance as a physical thing, such as a garden gnome.
   Remove the gnome from your mind and set it on the floor in front of you.
Circulate the gnome clockwise, then counterclockwise.

Once you've completed this, you'll have a basic knowledge of how your scenario seems from every perspective, 360 degrees around. As a result, you will be in a position to make judgments that will unify rather than divide everyone concerned.

How Perspective Influences Your Emotions

"If you change how you think about it, your feelings and actions will change."

This quote is a good, neat distillation of the whole concept of adjusting your viewpoint, and hence of this article. By definition, seeing anything from the "other" side means changing how that thing affects your life. Mischel is implying that the simple act of *looking at it differently* may be all that is required to achieve this.

Are you arguing with your supervisor about when that important project should be ready for presentation? They claim the leadership meeting is next week, while you say the shareholder meeting is two weeks later. Instead of sticking to your guns, take a step back and consider the situation from their point of view. You may discover that doing a dry run for the leadership group is advantageous, especially because you'll have two weeks to make modifications and refine your presentation before it becomes public.

In many respects, this is related to being anchored in the present moment. When you get caught up in defending your point of view, what you're doing is concentrating on the future —and just one potential future at that. What you're witnessing is an additional two weeks of procrastination, of being able to concentrate on activities other than the project presentation. When you halt, take a step back, and look at the problem from every angle, you return to the present moment.

This is what allows you to change your viewpoint to that of your supervisor and observe the immediate consequences of your actions.

Staying concentrated on your side of the topic (argument) means remaining focused on just one potential result. Seeing an alternative may be immensely beneficial in many aspects of daily life. From work to commuting to inquiring how your partner's day went (or knowing when not to ask). Even if it's just falling on the sofa in front of repeats after dinner, playing a board game with the family, reading a book, or going for a nice stroll around the neighborhood.

All of this is from the relatively simple act of pausing, being present, and adjusting your viewpoint.

13

Chapter 13

Identifying and utilizing personal strengths

What do you excel at?

That is a question we all want to know about ourselves, as is the one that sometimes follows it: What are you not good at?

If you don't know how to answer those questions about yourself, stay reading—I'll help you get to know yourself better.

When I was 14, I found a strength I didn't realize I had. My elder brother had bought a home gym, but there was one issue that could be summed up in three words: "Some assembly required."

My brother huffed out after a few hours of working together with very nothing to show for it, grumbling under his breath, and left me alone with the page of assembly instructions. I worked my way through each stage gradually until the gym was ready for use later that night.

That day, I realized I have a skill that my brother lacked at the time, which meant I had something valuable to contribute.

Identifying your talents and shortcomings isn't only an activity to make you feel good (or awful) about yourself if you're thinking about establishing a company. It's a process that will teach you how to be more effective at what you do and where you need to improve if you want to be successful.

1. To begin, make two lists.

I propose that you spend around 30 minutes alone generating two lists before using any other sources to assist you discover your strengths and shortcomings.

Your first list will be focused on your company or entrepreneurial objectives. "Skills Required to Succeed," for example.

Don't be concerned about whether you've considered every conceivable talent needed for your firm to flourish. This is intended to provide a high-level summary. Depending on your industry, it might include phrases like "market understanding," "business development," "website development," or "product expertise." Once you've finished your list, highlight the talents you currently have and place a star next to the ones you believe you'll need to improve. Set this list aside for now; you'll return to it later.

The following list will demand you to be fully honest about yourself. You may make two columns, one for "Strengths" and one for "Weaknesses."

Depending on your personality, one of these columns will be much simpler to complete. I can only advise you to do your hardest to be impartial. Don't berate yourself for what you perceive to be serious defects, and don't exaggerate your abilities. Simply jot them down and move on.

You don't even need a complete list of 100 strengths and weaknesses. If you've added more than 10-15 things in each column, you're focusing too much on insignificant qualities and short- comings.

Examples of what you may add to this list include characteristics of your personality, such as "calm under pressure" or "achievement-driven," as well as technical talents, such as "HTML expertise" or "project management experience."

The goal of this list is to start with some broad thoughts about yourself and then obtain feedback from various sources to help you develop your list.

Try asking yourself questions like these to help you think about what to put in your strengths and weaknesses:

What do I excel at?

What have other people said about me?

What have people had to assist me with on several occasions?

What undertakings and activities seem to sap my energy?

Which projects have I worked on for hours without tiring?

What are my interests, and why do I like them?

After you've honestly assessed your strengths and limitations, it's essential to get feedback from individuals closest to you: a significant other, a mentor, close friends, or family members.

2. Consult with individuals you trust.

The issue with utilizing a list of your strengths and faults is that you have a skewed view of yourself. Most individuals place too much or too little value on themselves.

If you're anything like me, you manage to do both at the same time. We all need some kind of "sounding board" to assist us in gaining clarity and getting closer to the truth about ourselves. That's where other folks can help.

Consider three to five individuals whose views you value and who have lived or worked with you for a long length of time. You want individuals who have seen your character and conduct in a variety of settings. Most individuals will have a significant partner, maybe a mentor or adviser, a close friend, one or more siblings, or their parent(s).

The duration of your partnerships is not the only factor to consider. The most significant factor is whether you regard or believe their assessment of you. Some friends and family members will be too biased—they will either believe everything you do is fantastic or will have previously nasty and detrimental beliefs. Choose individuals who have a proven track record of being fair and helpful, even when they have had to tell you something you didn't want to hear.

Once you've chosen a group of individuals, contact them. You may meet them for coffee or just write an email with some questions and request honest feedback.

When you contact them, make sure you explain why you're asking for their feedback. Tell them you want to establish a company and that you're attempting to assess your strengths and shortcomings to be successful. Inquire about what aspects of your personality they believe will contribute to your success. Then, ask them to identify your shortcomings that might lead to failure.

Begin adding additional information to your two lists as you get comments. Some of the qualities and flaws you stated will be validated by others you trust, while others will be less important to those who have spent time with you.

3. Experiment with new things

One issue with distinguishing strengths and shortcomings arises when you lack experience. In certain circumstances, you may realize that your list of shortcomings primarily consists of "I don't know, I've never tried." For example, how can you tell whether you have athletic or artistic skills if you've never attempted something athletic or creative?

I'm a firm believer in challenging oneself to improve by trying new things. To be honest, if you're afraid to attempt new things, your quick personality test answer is: don't be an entrepreneur.

However, if you want to try new activities to figure out your skills and limitations, here are some options that won't take much time or money:

Experiential learning in the arts:

Painting/Drawing: Get a brush, some inexpensive paints, and some paper (or a canvas), and watch a YouTube lesson video.

Singing: You may have avoided karaoke bars in the past, but overcome your fear of shame and sing some of your favorite songs.

Dancing: Once again, YouTube will come in helpful, since there are plenty of dancing lesson videos available. You may practice in the seclusion of your own home until you believe you've mastered the dance.

film: We live in an extraordinarily exciting time in which many of us have the fundamental technology needed to create a film of movie-grade quality in our pockets. Make a 15- or 30-second film with one main goal in mind: to elicit an emotional reaction from your audience.

Cooking: Use a cookbook, Allrecipes, or another YouTube video to follow a recipe. Make a dinner that you've liked at a restaurant but have never attempted to make at home. You could be astonished to discover a talent that will also save you money.

Open mic evenings at comedy clubs are popular in many places. Are you feeling brave? Try writing a five-minute set of jokes and performing them in front of total strangers (pro tip: bring some pals for moral support).

4. Look for hints in your attempts and failures.

The aim is that as we get older, we will become more self-aware. Why? As we go through life on one path, we should gain certain lessons via the process of attempting and failing. After my first lover crushed my heart, I saw how strong love could be. After being dismissed from a job, I realized how much I valued a consistent salary. After my first serious vehicle accident, I learned how to be a better driver.

Failure is an essential component of achieving long-term success in any endeavor.

Through our failures, we grow more able to anticipate future threats and embed those lessons into the fabric of our being, allowing us to benefit from what were once losses. It is almost hard to notice these lessons amid a failure. It is only after the storm has gone that you can begin to piece together the jigsaw and discover the lesson to be learned in that scenario.

The important thing to remember is that in your failings, in your moments of failure, if you pay close attention, you might be able to start identifying the weaknesses in your own life that may have a hand in those failures, and if you are smart, you will start trying to learn how to minimize those issues and maximize what you are good at so that a path to success begins to emerge.

5. DISCUSS YOUR SUCCESSES

While failure may be a tremendous lesson, success breeds further success. Any experience, favorable or unpleasant, may be used as a teaching tool if the person is ready to use it. The trick, of course, is to jump right in and start looking for methods to obtain the essential expertise.

"You've got to put in your time," I hear so frequently at corporate firms, referring to the concept that you have to put in a particular number of years into a company before you start to see a positive correlation within your career.

6. KEEP HOLD OF YOUR IDENTITY

Whether you're attempting to be a good parent or a successful professional, you must have a firm grasp on your own identity. Knowing oneself will be critical to use those qualities and enjoy future success.

7. CONDUCT A STRENGTH TEST

If, after reading, you still have doubts about your abilities, you might consider taking a "strength test." These are intended to assist users in identifying their strengths, with the premise that our own particular biases may influence how we perceive our talents, and the test is supposed to help eliminate such prejudices.

How to Make the Most of Your Strengths
  The concept of using your strengths to leverage your skill set
   and drive yourself to success is something that we should all
think about and strive towards.

Consider a see-saw as an example of leverage. On a see-saw, one person often exerts all of their weight on one end of the see-saw, propelling the other person into the air. Similarly, if you used your qualities as the basis for your progress, you'd see a favorable link as your success grew.

MAKE AN INVESTMENT IN YOURSELF

Another factor to examine is how investing in yourself differs from investing in the stock market. Most experts will advise you to diversify your asset classes or invest in index funds when investing in the stock market so that you are not too concentrated on a single position that might drag down your portfolio.

When attempting to find and use your talents, you should adopt the exact opposite approach. When it comes to maximizing one's talents, you should try to put more of your time, energy, and money into a more narrowly focused move that strengthens your biggest strengths or skill set.

When looking at S&P benchmark performance year after year, I'd say that's a horrible technique for investing, but when it comes to your capabilities as a person, it's a wonderful approach.

Not only should you place your eggs in fewer baskets while focusing on your strengths, but also when working on your shortcomings. If you're great at communicating and maintain- ing connections but poor at sales, it seems to reason that you'd devote more effort to closing the deal.

RECOGNIZE AND IMPROVE YOUR WEAKNESSES

To harness your strengths, you should first identify any areas of weakness in your present body of work and then seek to strengthen those areas of weakness to build a stronger founda- tion for success.

You will achieve your goal of leveraging your strengths by minimizing your areas of weakness and increasing their strength. Reducing weakness helps you to perform at a better level as an individual and naturally gives greater power to the strengths that you have in your repertoire.

What exactly is the opportunity cost?

The word "opportunity cost" is most often employed in economic contexts, but it's also a good notion to consider when assessing your limitations. The principle is straightforward: given a restricted set of resources, opportunity cost indicates what you miss out on when you pick one option over another.

You only have a limited amount of time and money in this situation. Assume you have a "lack of sales ability" and "lack of accounting ability" marked as shortcomings. Is the advantage to you higher if you invest your time and money learning the abilities needed to become a better seller than if you use the same resources to build your accounting skills?

What are you going to do about the accounting deficiency if you examine those shortcomings and conclude that enhancing your sales abilities is more important? Another person's strength is another person's weakness. It's acceptable if you're not a natural at everything. Instead, do what you can and surround yourself with individuals who have qualities that balance out your limitations.

Many business owners see this as an "aha" moment for them.

Entrepreneurs often attempt to accomplish everything on their own and rapidly burn out. Their firm was able to become more productive and successful after they were able to bring in the correct person who could perform certain things better than them.

I hope you find these recommendations helpful as you attempt to determine your strengths and shortcomings. Is there anything else you'd want to add to my list? I'd love to hear about a moment when you uncovered a hidden strength or fought hard to overcome a shortcoming.

14

Chapter 14

Finding and aligning with personal purpose

Have you ever felt as though what you do is pointless? Like it doesn't matter or your effect on the world is negligible? For years, I felt this way and couldn't understand how everyone else seemed to have it all figured out from a young age. As a teenager and young man, I felt so inadequate that I essentially put myself into a box so that I could feel connected with something, recognize my contribution, and feel that what I was doing provided a purpose. While this method kept me occupied, I developed into a social chameleon, taking pride in my ability to blend in, go undetected, and adapt to any situation. While this seems to be a positive attribute, it comes at the expense of losing my basic identity and not understanding my mission in the world. When I think back on my adolescence and early twenties, I was mostly nervous and sad. I attribute much of my anxiety to two factors. 1) I was asking about the objective of the inquiry, and 2) I didn't have a response.

"Those who can clearly articulate their purpose, in my experience, have a higher quality of life, express more gratitude, and are generally happier."

What's the big deal about purpose...Is it really that important?

'Purpose' is an important aspect of my work, not just when coaching and mentoring people, but also when assisting organizations in aligning their culture with strategic aims. My emphasis on purpose is justified. Those who can clearly explain their purpose, in my view, have a higher quality of life, show more appreciation, and are generally happier.

Ok...So intent seems to be vital; please assist me in gaining clarity.

First and foremost, once you raise the question, there is no turning back. Simply throwing it out there and leaving the response fluttering in the air will not suffice. It requires purposeful and thorough attention to articulate your aim. I compare it to the process of unearthing a fossil. To disclose the complete fossil, use proper tools to gently extract the soil of the specimen while being cautious not to harm it. Patience and talent are required. If you speed up the process, you will likely skim over it and receive no clarity at all. If, on the other hand, you've courageously addressed the question about your mission but are having difficulty discovering it, here's a procedure I employ to assist individuals get clarity.

1) Discover your purpose via your values- What you most strongly value is often a good beginning point for discovering your mission. I usually begin with several Values Cards. First, lay them all out and divide them into two heaps. The first pile symbolizes your must-have values, whereas the second pile, although significant, does not connect as strongly with you. Turn your attention to the first pile and arrange them in descending order of importance, from most essential to least important. Now that you have your list ranked, you must narrow it down to the top 5 values...Even better, top three.

2) Articulate your purpose statement- Now that you've identified your top values, you should have a good idea of what your mission should sound like. At this point, don't worry about wordsmithing; instead, make a broad statement that encompasses the ideals with which you most strongly identify.

3) Test and simplify- Now that you have your values statement, it's time to condense it into a much more concise and punchy phrase. Remember that the goal of your mission statement is not to announce it to the whole world. It's a private affirmation for you to remind yourself of your values and what gives you energy. Simply stating your aim should arouse a great desire inside you to get started. You should feel emotionally connected to your mission. If you're having trouble, you can always run it by a few close friends or family members to obtain a second

opinion. You'd expect to hear "That's so you" or "Yes, you do that" from them. If they don't respond strongly, this is only a mirror of your emotional commitment to your objective. If you don't feel it, they won't either.

So I've got a mission statement... now what?

As you can see, establishing your mission statement requires a significant amount of effort. This is the simple part, without breaking your success bubble. Once you've determined your mission, you must reconcile who you are with what you do. To do so, consider how much of your time is spent aligned with your goal. What we describe as our purpose is often highly aspirational, representing a gap between who we are and who we aspire to be. Regardless of your employment, position, money, age, gender, or other characteristics, all prevalent knowledge says that we are at our best (in terms of how we feel about ourselves and how we affect the world) when we embody and live in harmony with our purpose.

But I'm content; why should I define my purpose?

Unfortunately, our culture feeds our insatiable desires for consumption, whether it be knowledge, entertainment, food, or resources. We are a mass populace that acts on instinct and seeks immediate fulfillment. The majority of my customers are confronting some kind of issue in terms of their purpose and contribution. Some describe this as emptiness about their objectives and having accomplished them, while others just feel like they are on a treadmill that has kept them focused on placing one foot in front of the other up until now. Above all, people are unhappy, but they can't articulate why.

My challenge to you is to see the importance of purpose before a terrible life catastrophe occurs. We've all been inspired by tales of great difficulty in which individuals overcame death, misfortune, and the constant battle to discover their purpose and create a more powerful life. Don't wait for death, difficulty, or hardship. Choose to live with a purpose today so that you may improve your life and have a good influence on others around you. While exaggerating one's sense of purpose may be regarded as a narcissistic exercise, I'd rather work toward narrowing the gap between who I am and who I want to be than live a shallow life filled with things I don't need, people I don't like, and doing activities that don't matter.

15

Chapter 15

Living a meaningful and fulfilling life

Have you ever considered how to have a meaningful life?

Perhaps you have a mental image of what this would look like. Maybe it's something you're already aiming towards. Perhaps the thought of achieving fulfillment leaves you perplexed and uncertain.

What, after all, does it mean to live a more fulfilled life? And how can we know what will fulfill us?

We may even doubt whether we can live a fulfilled life right now. So, whatever our current circumstances are, how can we find out what our secret formula for fulfillment is?

This article will provide you with some practical suggestions to help you figure out what a full life looks like for you. And, maybe most crucially, how to live it now!

What does it mean to have a fulfilled life?

So, what exactly does it mean to live a fulfilled life?

This is going to be different for every one of us. To be happy in life, we must first identify our purpose and ideals. Our own 'why' for life.

When we understand what inspires us, we may find fulfillment. When we devote our time and attention to what is most impor- tant to us.

A full existence entails much more than just being pleased in the present. Meaning is at the heart of a fulfilling existence. A meaningful life entails finding profound happiness in your work.

It's about feeling like you're being true to yourself as you go about your day. It is about being present at the moment and identifying the chances for fulfillment that are all around you.

We do not have control over every area of our existence. There are obstacles to overcome for every one of us. However, by focusing on living a full life, we may extract the most from each moment.

So, how can we live a meaningful life? Here are a few pointers to get you started.

How to Live a Meaningful Life

For every one of us, a fulfilling existence will seem different. Living a fulfilled life does not always need you to change your surroundings. However, you may opt to make some adjustments.

Leading a meaningful life is about your attitude toward life as much as it is about your surroundings. And having a sense of significance and purpose in our life may make even the most difficult situations bearable.

Each of us must uncover our secret formula for fulfillment. One that assists us in discovering what is significant to us, what makes us happy, and what aligns with our values. However, certain ideas may benefit us all.

Here are some ideas to help you discover your path to purpose and fulfillment, no matter what your circumstances are.

Make your priorities a top priority.

It's easy to get caught up in the hustle and bustle of daily life and lose sight of our priorities. We all need frequent chances to check in with ourselves and stay on course. To determine if the way we spend our time corresponds to our priorities.

Examining how we spend our days and comparing them to what is important to us may be eye-opening. But this journey of self- discovery isn't about berating ourselves.

Instead, consider it an opportunity. If you see a disconnect between how you spend your time and what fulfills you, you are already halfway to leading a more satisfying life.

Now that you know what will bring you greater fulfillment, you can start making tiny, consistent adjustments to make it happen.

This week, make an effort to include what is most important to you on your to-do list as often as what is essential.

It's all too easy for what's essential to fall through the cracks in our to-do lists, calendars, and lives.

Find significance in anything you do.

As we consider how to live a more satisfying life, we may begin to wonder whether fulfillment is attainable where we are right now. Do we need to make a career change to humanitarian work or start a world-changing side business?

Perhaps shifting employment is the best thing for you, or maybe that company is where you belong. However, significant adjustments are not required to attain fulfillment in your life.

Any work may provide fulfillment. It is just where you are right now. Identifying your values may assist you in making your job more meaningful now, regardless of your circumstances.

Perhaps you might broaden your responsibilities to incorporate other things that offer you a feeling of purpose. Perhaps when you consider your values, you will view your work from a new perspective.

Reduce your expectations.

It may sound contradictory, but one way to live a more meaningful life is to decrease your expectations! This does not imply that you should abandon your standards. Simply said, expecting perfection in every scenario might make us feel unsatisfied with our life.

When we have unrealistically high expectations, life might become a series of disappointments. Instead of concentrating on what is occurring, we may find ourselves wishing for what is not.

Being present at the moment is a crucial aspect of having a meaningful life. When we accept that life isn't flawless, we may be receptive to all of the wonderful things that are occurring right now.

Opportunities for a more meaningful existence may already exist around us, but our unreasonable expectations keep them hidden.

Make time to express thanks.

Living a fulfilled life is about how we see our current situation. Have we lost sight of the things that used to make us happy?

What is always around us might simply slip into the background. That is understandable. But when we stop seeing the beautiful things in life, we lose out on chances to feel satisfied.

Taking time to calm down and appreciate the little things in life might boost our feeling of fulfillment.

There are several methods to create a grateful attitude, and doing so may significantly improve our feeling of fulfillment in life.

Create a positive connection with yourself.

When we struggle with our connection with ourselves, it is difficult to feel fully satisfied in life.

We often devote so much of our energy in life to relationships with other people. We recognize the significance of these connections, but what about our relationship with ourselves?

A meaningful existence entails appreciating and caring for oneself. When we are drained or battling with negative self-talk, it may be difficult to find fulfillment.

We must have a good connection with ourselves to be genuinely satisfied.

Surround yourself with individuals who are 'good'.

The connections we surround ourselves with are another crucial aspect of having a fulfilled life.

Do the people around you make you feel good?

Are they motivating you to achieve your objectives?

Are your main connections a location where you build joyful memories?

Sometimes we need to take a step back and consider the people aroundus. Wemustmakeaconcertedefforttocultivate connections that strengthen us.

Good connections are necessary for feeling satisfied in life.

It's time to start living a more satisfied life.

Whatever your circumstances, you can have a meaningful life.

Taking the time to identify what gives you a feeling of meaning and purpose is essential for daily fulfillment.

There may be changes you need to do

for your life to feel more rewarding. However, having a meaningful life is as much about attitude as it is about circumstances.

Gratitude. Self-Relationship. Liberation from Perfection. All of these things may make life seem so much richer.

After all, isn't that what we're all looking for?